Private Rio

THE GREAT HOUSES AND GARDENS

Private Rio

THE GREAT HOUSES AND GARDENS

EDITED BY

Juan Pablo Queiroz and Tomás de Elia

INTRODUCTION AND TEXT BY

André Corrêa do Lago

WITH THE COLLABORATION OF

Roa Lynn

PHOTOGRAPHS BY

Tomás de Elia

RIZZOLI
NEW YORK

FRONTISPIECE
The Orleans e Bragança
House in Paraty.

First published in the United States of America
by Rizzoli International Publications, Inc.
300 Park Avenue South, New York, NY 10010
www.Rizzoliusa.com

ISBN: 0-8478-2474-8
LCCN: 2002090781

Project coordinator: Theresa Muniz
Captions translated form the Spanish by Anne Randle.

Designed by Ediciones Brambila, Buenos Aires.
Printed and bound in China

2003 2004 2005 2006 2007 / 10 9 8 7 6 5 4 3 2 1

Malta
Avenida Central
Rio 7-10-06

INTRODUCTION

A view of the old Avenida Central in 1907.

The Orleans e Bragança house in Paraty, built in the late seventeenth century.

"I HAVE ARRIVED in the most beautiful city in the world," writes Stefan Zweig about his trip to Rio, in 1941. The site of Rio de Janeiro, with its magnificent bay and beaches set against an abruptly rising mountain range, has stunned generations of inhabitants and travelers alike. Although it is difficult to find anyone who does not remember at least one image of Rio's dramatic landscape, very few people outside Brazil know that the city has an extraordinary history, which included serving as the capital of a nineteenth-century European Empire. It is not surprising, then, to discover that Rio contains some of the most important architecture on the continent, as well as many beautiful houses in and around the city.

COLONIAL RIO

Rio de Janeiro's first visitors arrived on January 1, 1502, as part of a Portuguese exploratory voyage that included Amerigo Vespucci. The crew believed they had entered the mouth of a river, hence the name, Rio de Janeiro or "River of January." In fact, the river was a 147-square mile bay, still known today by its Indian name, Guanabara, or "arm of the sea." Recognizing the area's economic value, a French fleet arrived in 1555 with the intention of founding France's first colony in the southern half of South America. It didn't take long for the Portuguese to become aware of the enemy's presence. The French were expelled, and from the 1560s onwards the Portuguese started building forts and simple constructions for a very limited community. While the Portuguese dominated the coast of Brazil from the Amazon delta to today's Uruguay, their colony was often attacked by the French, the Dutch, and the Spaniards. The bay of Rio had great strategic importance in helping the Portuguese colonizers maintain control over their immense possession.

The economic activity of colonial Brazil was, until the seventeenth century, concentrated primarily in the northeast, where sugar cane was grown. The capital of the colony was then Salvador, in what is now the state of Bahia. Although, at the time, Rio was a less important city, significant buildings for military and religious functions were built. Some of these, like the São Bento Monastery, are among the jewels of the Baroque.

The discovery of gold in the province of Minas Gerais, three hundred miles west of Rio, changed the city's fate. By the eighteenth century, mining was the main economic activity in the Brazilian territory. Thus the economic center of Brazil shifted from the northeast to Rio, the most important port city close to Minas. In 1763, Portugal recognized Rio's new status as the colony's leading city and transferred the capital from Salvador to Rio. To keep control of its overseas territory, the Portuguese kept it isolated from foreigners, forbidding any industry or economic activity that could diminish its dependence on its colonizer.

THE CAPITAL OF A EUROPEAN EMPIRE

The invasion of Portugal by Napoleon's troops in 1808 created the unprecedented situation of a colony becoming the seat of government for the mother country. The Portuguese court moved en masse to Rio, and the city became the capital of the Portuguese Empire. One can imagine the amazement of the 50,000 inhabitants of the city watching the arrival, in a few weeks, of more than 15,000 Portuguese noblemen and retainers who insisted on maintaining their own European court style, including dress, in the midst of the tropics. Although indignation was high when the occupants of hundreds of houses were expelled to accommodate the court, the economic opening that followed created opportunities that the former closed environment made impossible. The royal family moved to the Governor's Palace (known today as the Paço Imperial) located in the middle of the city, and later to the Quinta da Boa Vista, a country house in the suburbs surrounded by large gardens.

The fleeing Portuguese court moved with everything they could bring, from the contents of the Royal Library to fabulous French silverware designed in the eighteenth century by François-Thomas Germain for King José I. Determined to make the best of the situation, King João VI set about changing the nature of his new capital. Rio was suddenly thrust into a world of manners and elegance which transformed its character. João VI had actually arrived in Brazil as Prince Regent and, at the death of his mother, Queen Mary I, became in 1818 King of Portugal, Brazil, and the Algarves in a formal ceremony in Rio. Foreign visitors, who included diplomats, businessmen, artists, and scientists from different countries of Europe, were welcome in Brazil. Beautiful paintings and prints depicting the natural settings of the city made Rio famous around the world.

A view of the Quinta da Boa Vista. *Karl Robert von Planitz*, c. 1840.

After the arrival of the Portuguese court, the architecture of Rio switched from baroque to neoclassic, mostly due to the influence of Grandjean de Montigny, a French architect who arrived in Brazil in 1816 and stayed until his death in 1850. Rio had to mutate from the capital of a colony to the capital of the Portuguese Empire. This transformation required the construction of a large theater, a library, a botanical garden, and a hospital, as well as palaces, houses and various other buildings that the court deemed the indispensable symbols of power and culture. Schools, parks and banks sprouted across the city. New neighborhoods like Botafogo began to be occupied, bringing life to areas that were still inside the Bay, but closer to the sea.

King João VI thought his years in Brazil were the happiest in his life. In fact, he avoided returning to Europe for six years after Napoleon's defeat. Nevertheless, in 1821, after thirteen years in Brazil, political instability in Portugal forced him to return home. His son Pedro, heir to the Portuguese throne, remained in Rio and, one year later, declared Brazil's independence. He became Pedro I, Emperor of Brazil.

THE BRAZILIAN MONARCHY

From 1822 to 1889 Brazil was a constitutional monarchy. The country was viewed with some suspicion in the hemisphere, where nationhood was traditionally gained following wars of independence, and republics, not monarchies, were established. The Brazilian monarchy's strong links with European powers made it even more confusing: In 1817, Pedro I married Leopoldina von Hapsburg, the daughter of the Emperor of Austria. (She was the sister of Marie Louise, Napoleon's second wife). After Dona Leopoldina's death, Dom Pedro married Dona Augusta Amélia of Beauharnais, Duchess of Leuchtenberg, the niece of the King of Bavaria.

Dona Augusta Amélia, Empress of Brazil, with her daughter, Princess D. Maria Amélia.
Friedrich Dürck, date unknown.

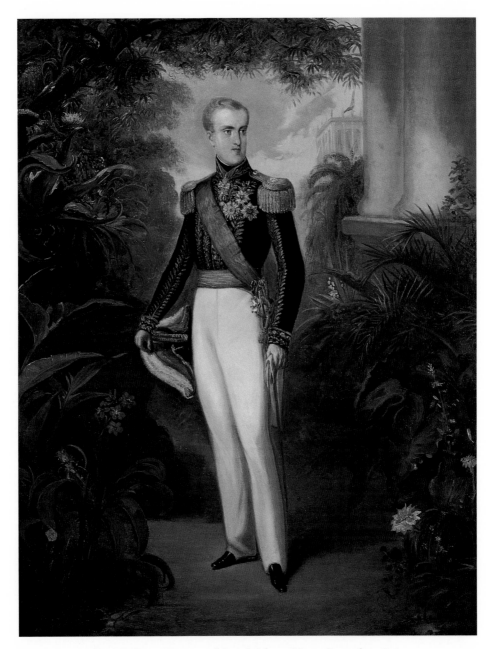

Dom Pedro II, Emperor of Brazil. *Johann Moritz Rugendas, 1846.*

When King João VI died, Emperor Pedro I of Brazil became titular king of Portugal as Pedro IV. However, shortly thereafter he conditionally abdicated the Portuguese throne in favor of his daughter. In 1831, facing internal pressure in Brazil and in view of a confusing dispute for the throne of Portugal, he decided to abdicate the Brazilian throne as well. He returned to Portugal and secured his daughter's claim against that of his brother. Before leaving Brazil, Pedro I turned the crown over to his five-year old son, Pedro II, who reigned in Brazil for fifty-eight years. Pedro II was a scholarly man, well traveled, and for four decades Brazil experienced domestic peace marked by steady progress and increasing contact with the outside world.

Rio preserves the most important monuments of the monarchy. The city expanded considerably and areas like Gloria, Catete, Santa Teresa, Laranjeiras, Cosme Velho and Jardim Botânico became the favorite places to build new houses, as the wealthiest part of the population avoided the increasingly unhealthy old town. Some of the best examples of residential architecture of the 1850s—the Palácio do Catete and the Palácio Itamaraty—are now museums. Meanwhile, a large area used in the first half of the nineteenth century for agriculture, mostly coffee, was transformed into what is now the largest urban forest in the world. The reforestation of the Floresta da Tijuca, from 1862 to 1891, was an extraordinary undertaking, since only trees and plants of the *Mata Atlântica*, the original vegetation of the Brazilian coast, were used.

The truly outstanding physical symbol of the monarchy was the summer capital—Petrópolis—built less than a hundred miles from Rio in the second half of the nineteenth century. Pedro II chose a location in the mountains, where the temperature is cooler than in Rio. The Imperial Palace and many of the houses built by members of the court clearly reflect a society that was trying to preserve the traditions of the *ancien régime*. Although the Brazilian monarchy was considered democratic by mid-nineteenth-century standards, it retained the most atrocious heritage of the colonial period—slavery. The economy of the country was still dependent on natural resources, mostly coffee and, for a few decades, rubber.

By the 1880s the monarchy was losing popular, political, and economic support. The dissatisfaction of the population with the consequences of a long and bloody war against Paraguay, the growing republican sentiment among the military, together with the dispute between those who supported and those who opposed slavery, which was abolished in 1888, all contributed to the fall of the Emperor. In 1889, Pedro II was deposed and asked to leave the country. He went into exile in France.

THE CAPITAL OF REPUBLICAN BRAZIL

The new regime was obligated to bring modernization to Brazilian society and, once again, the changes had to be visible in the capital. Baroque Rio was a creation of the colonial period; neoclassical buildings were the symbols of monarchy; now beaux-arts style was to reflect the new republican ideals. New buildings would not be enough. Massive urban intervention was then being undertaken in Europe and Rio had to follow the world's best and most modern example—the new Paris of Baron Georges-Eugène Haussmann, the greatest of the grand-scale city planners.

A beautiful boulevard—Avenida Central—was built, the old town was sanitized, large public parks were opened, and a "promenade" was created by the bay—the Avenida Beira Mar. All these changes were realized in a few years by a single mayor, Francisco Pereira Passos. Le Corbusier, who first visited the city in 1929, said of Rio: "...this other Haussmann

The Teatro Municipal and the old National School of Fine Arts, c. 1910.

has made the most dazzling township in the world… the city used to be timid, hidden in the hinterland. She has suddenly come to life."

A series of significant new buildings were also built in the first years of the twentieth century: an opera house—(the Teatro Municipal), the National Library, and the National School of Fine Arts. They were all inspired by French architecture and brought a Belle Époque ambience to the old town. Residential architecture was more adventurous and many Art Nouveau houses can still be found. Turn-of-the-century chateaux were also built, similar to ones found in New York or Buenos Aires. Two landmarks of residential architecture of the time are the Palácio Laranjeiras (1909), formerly the residence of the Guinle family and now the Governor's residence, and the house built in 1920 by Henrique Lage for his wife, Italian opera singer Gabriela Besanzoni, now an art school.

Rio paid a heavy price for some of its core modernization in the early part of the twentieth century. With space severely limited by the topography of the city, many sixteenth- and seventeenth-century structures, as well as elegant three and five-story buildings, were lost to the wrecking ball. In 1892 a tunnel was built that gave access to heart of Copacabana from the downtown side of the mountains. With the addition of a second tunnel in 1904, urbanization of Copacabana began in earnest as houses were built amongst the dunes. In historic terms, the neighborhoods of Rio facing the Atlantic ocean— Copacabana, Ipanema, Leblon—are all relative newcomers.

THE MODERN CITY

The growing conscience among Brazilian intellectuals in the 1920s that the country's culture was far from autonomous led to an extraordinary cultural movement. It opened broad new paths such as fascination with the country's unique heritage, the search for new values, and the rejection of the old European stereotypes. Brazilian painters, sculptors, musicians, and writers began to show an unprecedented originality at the same time that colonial art and architecture were being rediscovered. This redefinition of national culture coincided with a new political regime. In 1930 a victorious revolutionary movement headed by Getúlio Vargas gave power to politicians from different regions of Brazil who were more open to progress in industrialization, education and social justice.

Architecture was particularly bold in Rio de Janeiro, which saw, between 1936 and 1945, the construction of Brazil's first international architectural landmark, the Ministry of Education and Health (the architects were Lucio Costa, Oscar Niemeyer, Affonso Reidy, Jorge Moreira, Carlos Leão and Ernani Vasconcelos; Le Corbusier was a consultant). According to a 1943 article by Philip Goodwin, it was "the most beautiful government building in the Western Hemisphere … one of the finest buildings to be found in the world."[1] Within a very few years other important modern buildings were added to Rio's skyline, and this new generation of architects started building modern houses in many areas of the city. Garden design acquired new dimensions through the work of Roberto Burle Marx and became one of Brazil's most acclaimed contributions to twentieth-century art.

From the 1930s on, the standard elegant Brazilian interior no longer displayed French or English furniture, but rather eighteenth-century Brazilian colonial furniture and silver together with modern Brazilian paintings on the walls. It is quite interesting to see how Brazil maintained the Portuguese tradition of paying special attention to residential architecture and decorative arts. The Portuguese, in their more glorious years, could not rival neighboring Spain in painting, but in comparing elegant Portuguese and Spanish houses, one sees very clearly the superior Portuguese talent in domestic decorative design.

Two houses that perfectly reflect this spirit belonged to a single man—Raymundo de Castro Maya. Maya restored an old colonial *chácara* (country place) in Alto da Boa Vista in the Tijuca Forest and built, in Santa Teresa, a modern house. Both are now museums that preserve most of their original decoration. However, the Brazilian residential designs most widely known abroad are probably Oscar Niemeyer's extraordinary residence, built in 1952 on the Estrada das Canoas, and the magnificent garden that Burle Marx created for Odete Monteiro in Correas in 1948.

By the 1940s, the beach had become an essential part of the city's life, and tastes changed. More and more people preferred to move from houses in the middle of tropical gardens to apartments facing the bay—in Flamengo or Botafogo—or facing the sea, first in Copacabana, and later in Ipanema and Leblon. Also, by mid-century, *favelas* (shanty towns on the hills) became more and more visible. These sprawling cantilevered slums were becoming a landmark of the city. Some people insisted on viewing them romantically, almost as charming tarnished ornaments. But the spread of the *favelas* after the 1960s showed them to be what they really were— the most visible aspect of the social injustice that persisted in the city.

AFTER BRASÍLIA

In April 1960, Rio ceased to be the capital of Brazil. The new capital, Brasília, five hundred miles from the coast, had been designed and built in three years by two architects from Rio—Lucio Costa was responsible for the urban master plan and Oscar Niemeyer designed the striking official buildings. Debate on the consequences of the creation of Brasília still inflames *cariocas* (natives of Rio) who are divided between those who believe the city has suffered little, because it continues to have sufficient personality and economic importance, and those who are convinced Brasília was an anti-Rio move that seriously harmed the city's prospects.

The fact is that some aspects of Rio life changed considerably after the capital relocated to the interior. Local politics and regional issues became more important and a feeling of decreasing cosmopolitanism was palatable. The departure of foreign diplomats to the new capital led to the destruction of many of the most beautiful embassies in Rio, the former residences of traditional families. Fortunately, some of the embassies were preserved, outfitted with new functions. The British Embassy, for example, built in 1949, was so grand it became the mayor's office and was renamed the Palácio da Cidade.

Since 1960 the expansion of the city into former wilderness areas has been both surprising and staggering in scale. Suburbs like Barra da Tijuca have grown so much and so far from the traditional neighborhoods that most of the old symbols of the capital have little meaning to new generations. Rio has become many cities. From old houses on the mountains to modern penthouses by the beach, *cariocas* have a very wide choice of places to live and they can all praise the fact that they are close to nature. The city's denizens are well aware that Rio is the only mega-city in the world more famous for its natural setting than for its buildings. And that is why living with a view is an essential goal. There are many to choose from: views to the bay or to the beaches, to the large lake (Lagoa) that drains into the Atlantic, to the mountains, to the forest, or to the statue of Christ the Redeemer atop Corcovado.

Rio combines a unique mix of a large, pulsating city—metropolitan Rio has more than eight million inhabitants—with a lush holiday setting. Carnival, beaches, music and natural beauty have long been trademarks of Rio. Some would say that the loss of capital status has strengthened these aspects. But the often-reported violence on the city's streets and the visible social disparities evidenced by the *favelas* have stained Rio's reputation since the 1970s. Today Brazilian society is more conscious of its inequalities than ever before. Finding solutions to both social and environmental problems have engaged politicians and the population in general.

Cariocas, whatever their social class, are very proud of their city. Perhaps they are correct in their conviction that Rio is the most beautiful city in the world. Rio is still, as Paul Claudel, the French writer and diplomat, used to affirm, "the only large city that has not succeeded in expelling nature." It is fair to say that the houses in this book can be viewed through differing prisms—as reflections of an unequal society, but also as evidence of *carioca* originality, quality, and thoroughgoing familiarity with traditional and modern forms. These houses tell a partial but splendid story of a fascinating city renowned for its spectacular setting, its intense and varied cultural life, and its relaxed attitude toward pleasure.

1. "Brazil Builds for the New World". *California Arts and Architecture*, Feb. 1943.

THE HOUSES

The Guanabara Bay viewed from the Monteiro de Carvalho's garden.

A COLONIAL HOUSE IN GLÓRIA

Surrounded by tropical vegetation and located behind the church of *Nossa Senhora da Glória do Outeiro*, this house maintains traces of the original eighteenth-century building. The stained glass above the windows and the wrought iron lamp holders on the facade, reflect the nineteenth-century interventions in the house.

I T IS EASY TO UNDERSTAND why foreign artists who visited Rio de Janeiro in the nineteenth century were inspired to paint the hill of Gloria. This location reunited the exotic themes that made Brazil so attractive to Europeans: luxuriant vegetation on a mountain by the sea dominated by an exquisite baroque church. Today, on reaching the top of the hill, the first impression is of a village. But, very quickly, the splendid views remind the observer that the neighborhood is in the middle of a large modern city. This property, located right behind the church of *Nossa Senhora da Glória do Outeiro*, with a colonial house surrounded by a tropical garden, nevertheless restores the first impression.

The house was built in the late eighteenth century, and considerably enlarged in the 1880s, responding to both Baroque and neoclassical influences. A new house was built next to it in the 1960s, with original materials collected from the demolition of colonial houses in downtown Rio. The garden, divided by the two houses, has a privileged position; one part overlooks Guanabara Bay, the other overlooks Corcovado, crowned with the statue of Christ the Redeemer.

Two sisters brought to this place a unique feeling of quality and understatement. Their father, Oswaldo Aranha, was one of the most respected public figures in Brazil—a former Ambassador to the United States, Minister of Foreign Affairs, and President of the United Nations General Assembly. Both sisters married diplomats, and both lived in various Brazilian Embassies throughout the world, including London, Washington, Rome and Paris.

Their many years abroad strengthened their conviction that a Brazilian house, like Brazil itself, can mix influences without losing its own identity. When they eventually returned to live in Rio, the sisters asked architect Wladimir Alves de Souza and garden designer Roberto Burle Marx to assist them in creating a place where their large families would feel at home. According to their friend, Fleur Cowles, who visited them all over the world, "when I came to Gloria, I had the feeling they could never have lived anywhere else."

Inside the hall with its seventeenth-century Spanish furniture is *A Vision of Saint Antonio de Pádua,* painted between 1646 and 1652 by the Spanish artist Alonso Cano. The eighteenth-century silver candlesticks are Italian.

The elegant dining room is decorated with panoramic wallpaper, the work of Jean Julien Deltil (1781–1853) and printed by Zuber et Cie, Rixheim, France. It represents views of Brazil based on lithographs of the Bavarian artist Johann Moritz Rugendas (1802–1858).

THE GUINLE PAULA MACHADO HOUSE

Architect Armando da Silva Telles built
this house in 1910 for Celina Guinle and
her husband, Linneo de Paula Machado.

RIGHT
The beaux-arts style entrance hall of the
magnificent Guinle Paula Machado residence.

In the dining room, a late seventeenth-century painting by the Dutch painter Jan Weenix.

LEFT
The living room looks as though it had been brought over from a lovely Parisian residence. Count Robert de Montesquiou-Fezensac, today remembered as one of the models for the Baron de Charlus, the character in Proust's *Remembrance of Things Past*, introduced the painter Paul-César Helleu to Celina de Paula Machado. Helleu made various paintings for the family, among them the portrait of Celina, now in this room.

IN THE FIRST DECADES of the twentieth century the Guinle family was responsible for the construction of mansions, hotels and apartment buildings that became landmarks of Rio de Janeiro. Many of these buildings still exist, like the Copacabana Palace Hotel, the Palácio Laranjeiras (today the Governor's residence) and this house, located in the district of Botafogo. It was designed in 1910 by the architect Armando da Silva Telles, inspired by the École des Beaux Arts in Paris. This was a time when the elite of the Americas—from New York to Buenos Aires—turned to elegant houses in Europe as models for residences in their own countries. The project was commissioned by Candido Gaffré, an old friend of the Guinle family, as a wedding present for Linneo de Paula Machado and Celina Guinle.

This wedding, one of the major social events in Brazil at the beginning of the century, united two highly influential families in Rio de Janeiro and São Paulo whose businesses ranged from banks to farming and from ports to utilities. Linneo was a famous figure also in Paris, where he spent at least four months a year at his *hôtel particulier* on the Rue de Grenelle in the 1910s. As the son of an important industrialist, he was the archetypal millionaire who found that Paris met his tastes in every way. His passion for horse racing led him to create Rio's Jockey Club Brasileiro. The track, built in 1926, is reputed to be among the most beautiful in the world. Celina's portrait by Helleu and a caricature of Linneo by Sem reflect how much the couple dominated the codes of the *grand monde*.

The Ball organized in this house in 1922 to celebrate the centenary of Brazil's independence, was considered for years to have been the most elegant party ever held in Rio de Janeiro. The house, still inhabited by descendants of the Guinle-Paula Machado marriage, is one of the few in this district to have survived the demolitions of the 1960s and 1970s and to have conserved its large garden. Fortunately, over the years, no decorator saw fit to strip the interior of its beaux-arts spirit. The São Clemente house preserves its original style.

In this room are displayed family photographs and objects recalling
the passion of Linneo de Paula Machado for horse racing.

RIGHT
The hall preserves the original decoration of a house that hosted
memorable social events for Brazilian high society.

In the bedroom sector, another family portrait painted
by Paul-César Helleu, and furniture brought from Paris in 1910.

LEFT
Family souvenirs in a room now used for storage.

The kitchen with its marble furniture and walls covered
with French tiles remains unchanged.

SÍTIO COCHRANE

On a bridge that crosses the lake, a bench covered
with old Portuguese tiles. The garden, created in the
second half of the nineteenth century by its owner,
William Cochrane, conserves its original layout.

RIGHT
The house, built in the 1930s in the district of Alto
da Boa Vista, was the last neo-colonial project by
the great Brazilian architect, Lucio Costa.

MANY OF THE DISTINGUISHED VISITORS to Sítio Cochrane refer to it as the most beautiful property in Latin America. Although superlatives are dangerous, it is difficult not to be overwhelmed by the beauty of this place apparently lost in a tropical forest, surrounded by mountains. Whereas in fact, a simple ride to Ipanema from Alto da Boa Vista—as this neighborhood is known today—takes less than fifteen minutes.

When British Admiral Thomas Cochrane, later Lord Dundonald, received this property as a gift from Emperor Pedro I in the 1820s, the land was almost barren, spoiled by decades of coffee planting. Cochrane had taken part in Brazil's brief war of independence and subsequently returned to Europe. Before leaving Brazil he gave the land to his cousin, William Cochrane, who built a large house and, by the 1860s, created a garden that mixed British gardening traditions with tropical native plants.

In 1930, Ernesto and Maria Cecilia Fontes bought this property, which by then was in a serious state of decay. They preserved the garden's original design and asked architect Lucio Costa to create a new house. At the time Costa was one of the young intellectuals who were fighting for the preservation of Brazil's architectural heritage. He had already designed a few houses in Rio in a neocolonial style. Shortly after submitting the plan for a beautifully proportioned house inspired by colonial *fazendas,* he decided to propose a radically modern design. This was a turning point in Costa's career—the architect was to become known worldwide as the founder of the Brazilian modern movement.

The Fontes favored the neocolonial project, which had a natural link to the Sítio Cochrane's history and to the magnificent garden design. Architect César Mello e Cunha executed the project, since Costa refused to build what he called his "last eclectic-academic manifestation." Costa's modern proposal would certainly have become an international landmark. But the house built by the Fontes, where their daughter still lives with her family, nevertheless has the power of perfection: nothing can be added or excluded without spoiling the result.

The house has a view of a magnificent tropical landscape, with the Pedra Aguda rising behind.

The bridge crossing the lake. The layout
of the garden combines the rigorous
tradition of the European landscaping
with the exuberance of tropical vegetation.

In the garden, a hidden corner dominated by huge ferns.

LEFT
The stone steps lead to the swimming pool that is fed
by the streams flowing through the property.

White lilies growing beside the lake.

RIGHT
This beautiful stairway leading up to the house,
is one of the many surprises of the garden.
The stones on the wall are covered with silver ferns.

THE GEYER HOUSE

A small bridge over the Carioca river leading
to a garden of azaleas.

RIGHT
This old eighteenth-century coffee farmhouse
is backed by the magnificent Corcovado hill,
crowned by the statue of Christ the Redeemer.

W HEN RIO DE JANEIRO BECAME THE CAPITAL of colonial Brazil, late in the eighteenth century, the city already contained a considerable number of beautiful church-es and monasteries. The city flourished as gold found in Minas Gerais—three hundred miles west of the coast—was shipped to Portugal through Rio's port. By the 1780s, coffee growing had also become an important economic activity around the city and large *fazendas* (farmhouses) were built.

The Geyer house was originally one of these *fazendas* sur-rounded by coffee trees. It is located beneath the Corcovado mountain in Cosme Velho, now a residential area in the middle of the city. Most of the neighboring country houses have disappeared, like the residence of Henry Chamberlain, the British Consul in Rio from 1815 to 1829. This diplomat is remembered by collectors thanks mostly to his son, Henry, who in 1822 published, in London, the very prized volume of prints and aquatints entitled *Views and Costumes of the City of Rio de Janeiro*. Today only about one hundred copies exist, one of which is in the library of this house.

Paulo and Maria Cecília Geyer put together what is probably the largest and most comprehensive collection of books, maps, paintings, drawings and prints related to the city of Rio de Janeiro. One could hardly find a more suitable house for such a collection, which was eventually enriched by important items that belonged to the Soares Sampaios, Maria Cecília's family, one of the most tradi-tional in Brazil. The furniture and objects are faithful to the house's spirit—most were made by Brazilian and Portuguese artisans in colonial times, or during the monarchy.

As in many other mountainous areas that exist within Rio, the garden of this house seems to merge into the forest, which was re-planted with native trees and vegetation in the late nineteenth century, after decades of use for agriculture. Paulo and Maria Cecília Geyer have decided that this residence, with its extraordinary col-lection and garden, will be donated after their death to the Imperial Museum of Petrópolis.

In a garden nook, a traditional nineteenth-century Portuguese ceramic statue.

RIGHT
This room hosts a collection of outstanding pieces of iconography related to Rio de Janeiro, among which the painting entitled *Igreja da Glória, Morro do Castelo e Praia de Santa Luzia* by Friedrich Hagedorn, c. 1860.

In the dining room, the *Compagnie des Indes* porcelain ordered by the Viscount of Itamaraty. The Dom José style chairs and the table have belonged for generations to the Soares Sampaio family. The nineteenth-century silver candlestick was created for a home in the city of Olinda, to the North of Brazil.

LEFT
Two views of the Guanabara Bay painted in 1830 by Sunqua, the only Chinese artist to paint Brazilian landscapes in the nineteenth century.

In the library, some of the most significant works on Brazil published between the seventeenth and nineteenth centuries. On the right, views of the cities of Salvador and Manaus.

LEFT
A copy of the book *Historia Naturalis Brasiliae*, edited by Laet in 1648, which tells the story of one of the first scientific expeditions to visit Brazil. The candlestick belonged to the Emperor Dom Pedro II of Brazil.

A House in Santa Teresa

The entrance pathway to the house
of Viviane Soares Sampaio.

RIGHT
Lunch in the courtyard. The house was built
with materials from old buildings that had been
demolished in Rio between 1930 and 1950.

A waterfall brings water directly
to the pool from the Carioca river.

LEFT
A corner of the veranda.

THE HILL OF SANTA TERESA, located next to Rio's business district, is probably the most charming neighborhood in the city. All kinds of people live there—bohemians, businessmen, intellectuals, artisans and artists, rich and poor—and they are all unconditional in their devotion to its magic. A visitor who comes back to Santa Teresa after a few years will be amazed to see how little it has changed. This has been true for the last thirty years, which makes it a unique place in Rio. The neighborhood has so much personality that it has almost become an island in the middle of the city, a place where the characteristics of a Rio of decades past still survive with such things as a tramway, long disappeared from the centre of the city.

Nineteenth-century engravings show there were already, at that time, a great many properties on the hill. However, the hill's advantages have been appreciated as far back as the eighteenth century, not only for climatic reasons, but also because of the fresh water provided by the river that crossed the area flowing down the Floresta da Tijuca.

The house where Viviane Soares Sampaio lives was built by her maternal grandparents, Emilio and Valeria Bidisnig, who arrived in Rio in 1929 from Italy. On their first visit to the district, they were seduced by its charm and beauty and decided to build their new home there. Together they collected materials from houses that were being demolished downtown and used them for their new-old house. In 1959 they considered their residence finished.

Viviane moved to the house in 1980 and set up an antique shop on the first floor. As often happens in Rio, no matter how attractive the interior, one is first seduced by the views. After awhile, however, one can't help but appreciate the house's interior. Important art works by Brazilian and foreign artists live peacefully with eighteenth-century furniture that belonged to generations of the Soares Sampaio family. Viviane's eclectic but sure taste fits perfectly with the house and the neighborhood, where building styles vary from colonial to Art Deco, from neo-medieval to neoclassical.

59

The house contains pieces from different periods and different
countries. The seventeenth-century carving of São Miguel de Botas
is a work from the Jesuit missions in the south of Brazil.

LEFT
In the living room, family photographs and a small sculpture
by Sérgio Camargo. On an old rosewood table, are three portraits
of musicians, the work of the German artist Harry Elsas (1954)
and a portrait of Viviane Soares Sampaio painted
by Abdul Mati Klarwein in 1979.

In the dining room, two Portuguese ceramic figures from the Santo Antônio do Porto factory and a Dona María style column. The stone sideboard was once the base of a balcony in an old house of Rio de Janeiro.

RIGHT
The living room overlooks the Guanabara Bay.

THE MOREIRA SALLES HOUSE

The main entrance to the house built in
the district of Gávea in 1950 by the architect
Olavo Redig de Campos.

RIGHT
A view of the imposing gallery. Traditional
elements in colonial architecture in Brazil
were adapted in an original way for this
modern project.

T HERE ARE FEW VERY LARGE HOUSES anywhere that have successfully combined monumentality with modern architecture. Many good architects have failed in this attempt. This grand house in the Gávea section of Rio is an exception. Architect Olavo Redig de Campos designed it in 1950 for Walther Moreira Salles, then a prominent banker, who was later Brazil's Minister of Finance and twice Ambassador to the United States.

Redig de Campos was born in Rio but received his degree in architecture in Rome, in 1931. Moreira Salles recognized the architect's broad culture and was impressed by his sense of scale. Redig de Campos presented several architectural options to his client—including a neocolonial version. Moreira Salles chose to develop the modern alternative.

The property, divided by a creek, is located in an area where the Atlantic forest is still well preserved. The owner intended that a garden, rather than mountains or the ocean, provide interesting views. Roberto Burle Marx attacked the grounds project with brio. The plan of the house was organized around a patio, where rare Brazilian trees were planted. The reception areas open onto the patio and to a large, partially covered terrace. All the bedrooms overlook the forest, in the section of the house closest to the creek, which assures fresh temperatures and the constant sound of flowing water.

In the 1960s the house was extensively redecorated. While respecting its architecture, one of the best collections of Brazilian colonial furniture was integrated with European art, including sculptures by Matisse and Giacometti and two seventeenth-century Gobelin tapestries from the *Nouvelles Indes* series. The interiors attained an opulence never surpassed in Rio. The house was used extensively for entertaining illustrious visitors. Recently it has been restored to its original modernist spirit and is now a private cultural center, maintained by the Moreira Salles family.

An old Portuguese fountain in the courtyard. The undulating roof links the entry hall to the bedroom sector.

RIGHT
The Portuguese tiles on the walls of this room and the Indo-Portuguese mother of pearl *secrétaire* are all of the eighteenth century.

TOP
The swimming-pool pavilion was built
in the early 1970s.

RIGHT
This corner of the pool shows the integration
of the modern garden with the native vegetation.

LEFT
The garden was designed by Roberto Burle Marx
and includes a group of "pau-mulato" trees,
native to the Amazon.

A pool with a tiled wall, designed by Burle Marx in 1949.
The tiles are another example of traditional Portuguese
architectural elements adapted to this residence.

This part of the garden can only be reached by crossing the reception rooms. Burle Marx and Redig de Campos designed this terrace garden to be seen from the house as an abstract work of art.

AN APARTMENT IN IPANEMA

This penthouse, on the avenue Vieira Souto,
occupies three floors of a building designed by
Oscar Niemeyer in 1960. He also designed the
staircase leading up to the terrace.

RIGHT
The structure of the pavilion was designed by
Niemeyer so as not to interfere with the view
of the beach.

IF EVERY NEIGHBORHOOD OF RIO reflects a particular moment of its history, Ipanema represents the 1960s at its best. The area was not overpopulated; it attracted young people; there were no large hotels; tourism and shopping were still very much concentrated in Copacabana; a city ordinance did not allow new buildings facing the sea to exceed six floors. Rio owes its reputation for a relaxed and sexy way of life largely to Ipanema. The hit song, "Girl from Ipanema," by Antonio Carlos Jobim and Vinicius de Moraes, made this beach famous all over the world.

The most exclusive apartment buildings in Rio since the sixties are located on Avenida Vieira Souto, facing Ipanema beach. This penthouse occupies the top three floors of a six-story building on Avenida Vieira Souto, designed in 1960 by Oscar Niemeyer, Brazil's most famous architect. Niemeyer gave special attention to the project because one of its residents would be Brazilian President Juscelino Kubitschek, who had given him some of the commissions that secured his international reputation. Although Niemeyer was born in Rio and still lives there, some of his most influential works were built in Belo Horizonte (Pampulha) and in Brasília, when Kubitschek was respectively mayor of Belo Horizonte and President of Brazil.

Niemeyer was convinced there could not be a better reason for a building to have a glass curtain wall than to face a beautiful beach. He eliminated any structural element that would disturb the views. The apartment's top floor is a prolongation of the beach, almost as if it were a pavilion. The young business woman who now lives in this penthouse respected the building's original architecture and combined excellent pieces of Brazilian art with modern furniture. The tone is set by the proximity to street level. The ambience also symbolizes in a way how close Brazilian culture is to its popular roots. This apartment is an ode to the sea and to Ipanema's way of life.

The apartment has a panoramic view of the beaches of Ipanema and Leblon, and of the *Dois Irmãos* hill.

RIGHT
The living room was decorated to harmonize with the original architecture. Works of great Brazilian artists such as Antônio Bandeira, Iberê Camargo and Manabu Mabe share the space with modern furniture like this couch by Mies van der Rohe.

THE MELLO FRANCO NABUCO HOUSE

The house, built in 1937 for Maria do Carmo and
José Nabuco, lies at the foot of Corcovado hill.

RIGHT
This room reflects the sobriety and elegance of a
traditional Brazilian home. The portrait of Joaquím
Nabuco, at the age of eight, was painted in 1857.

The entrance stairway leads up to the living room on the second floor. The objects and furniture were collected by the Mello Franco and Nabuco families and include such variations as a painting from Cuzco and a nineteenth-century sunshade for religious processions.

LEFT
In the living room, on an eighteenth-century sideboard, is a small portrait of Francisco Manoel de Mello Franco, who moved to Brazil with the Portuguese royal family in 1808.

CULTURE AND POLITICS are the two ingredients that define the spirit of this house located in the district of Botafogo. It was built in 1937 by José Nabuco, a prominent lawyer, and his wife, Maria do Carmo de Mello Franco Nabuco, one of Rio's mythical power couples for more than five decades. This was a place where every guest was sure to have a memorable time meeting politicians, businessmen and artists from all over the world.

Maria do Carmo's family, the Mello Francos, arrived in Brazil in 1808, when the Lisbon court, owing to the Napoleonic wars, followed the Portuguese monarch to the new capital of the kingdom: Rio de Janeiro. They stayed in the country and were active in politics throughout the century. José's father, Joaquim Nabuco, became one of the country's most remarkable politicians in the second half of the nineteenth century when he was the leader of the movement against slavery in Brazil. Subsequently, he became Brazil's Ambassador to the United States.

This house contains many pieces of furniture and portraits of the couple's ancestors, handed down from generation to generation for more than two centuries. Cândido Portinari painted the portraits of Maria do Carmo and her children, as well as the three magnificent paintings in the dining room, which he wanted to be frescoes. But José asked him to paint them on canvas so the wall would not "become more valuable than the house itself." Portinari was at the height of his career, executing monumental works for the United Nations Building in New York and the Library of Congress in Washington, D.C. In 1943, The Museum of Modern Art in New York organized a retrospective of his work.

Other important artists were involved in the design of this house, such as landscape designer Roberto Burle Marx, yet no attempt was made to make the residence feel overwhelming or impressive. José and Maria do Carmo wanted their guests to feel at home. But as it was their home, every element had to have quality or historical relevance. Most *cariocas* would agree that the Mello Franco-Nabuco house is the archetypal Brazilian elegant home.

A portrait of Maria do Carmo Nabuco painted
in 1937 by Cândido Portinari.

RIGHT
The magnificent service of *Compagnie des Indes*
porcelain contributes to the elegance of the
dining room. The three paintings are by Portinari.

The garden, an early work by Roberto Burle Marx,
incorporates traditional elements.

RIGHT
A common sight in this house, which is close
to unspoiled areas of natural vegetation in the
Atlantic Forest on Corcovado hill.

THE MONTEIRO DE CARVALHO HOUSE

A row of imperial palm trees in front of the house. The property occupies a large portion of the hill of Santa Teresa.

RIGHT
The large gallery is one of the spaces used most frequently by the family. In the foreground, a sculpture of Auguste Rodin.

THE TOP OF SANTA TERESA HILL is occupied by this large property which has some of the most beautiful views of Rio de Janeiro. Alberto and Beatriz Monteiro de Carvalho bought the house in 1938. They knew there was no other place in Rio where they could have such a large garden, except in areas distant from downtown. The house was expanded and the interiors were completely redesigned. Beatriz used a fantastic combination of plants she found on the property, chosen by an Austrian botanist who had owned the place for many years, to create a completely new garden.

Monteiro de Carvalho was a key figure in the Brazilian business world, but he and Beatriz were more famous for their wide range of interests, strong personalities and immense generosity. They entertained frequently but seldom left their house, except for long trips to Europe and the United States. Alberto, who was trained as an architect, created an important library of architecture in his home, constantly enriched by the latest publications.

In spite of the couple's enthusiasm for the modern movement—they were close friends of Le Corbusier, whom they invited to Rio for a series of memorable lectures in 1929—they did not try to transform their house into an architectural landmark. They preferred to create a rather neutral décor for their exceptional objects and furniture. Art Nouveau and Art Deco decorative arts were their main interest. The house contains masterpieces, some of them custom-made for the house, by Gallé, Lalique, Daum, Tiffany and many other artisans. But the greatest treasure in the collection consists of a very rare and beautiful set of Gallé glasses with views of Rio de Janeiro.

Joaquim Monteiro de Carvalho, their son, continued to expand the family business. He lives in this house with his wife, Evinha. Some members of the family, including niece and nephew Beatriz and Olavo Monteiro de Carvalho, built separate houses on the same property. Although an avid collector himself, Joaquim decided not to change the interiors his parents had created, thereby preserving this house as one of the most outstanding 1930s décors ever created.

The stairway leading to the bedroom quarters.
The banisters were made in Rio de Janeiro
by the prestigious firm Laubisch, Hirth & Co.

RIGHT
A crystal table, an exclusive model by René Lalique
dating from the 1930s, dominates the hall. The lamps
are by Jean Perzel and Lalique. The arrangement for
the Baccarat flowerpot is composed of plants and
flowers from the garden. In the room at the back is
a portrait of Evinha Monteiro de Carvalho.

The dining room displays an outstanding crystal lamp by Lalique, specially designed for this residence.

LEFT
The library has some of the best examples of works published on Brazil in the nineteenth century. The Art Deco sculpture in bronze and ivory is the work of the Austrian artist Bruno Zach.

The master iron cabinet-maker, Raymond Subes, designed the
furniture in this room for the Monteiro de Cavalho family in
Paris, during the decade of the 1930s. The appliqués are by
Jean Perzel and the sculpture by Mauirce Guiraud-Rivière.

The gallery leading to the garden, with one of the
finest views of the Pão de Açúcar.

An Apartment in Copacabana

In the entrance hall, covered in black marble
from Bahia, stands a sculpture by Sérgio Camargo.

RIGHT
A view of the living room. Over the Dom José
style tables hangs a painting by Bernard Buffet
and another by Paul Jenkins.

C OPACABANA WAS THE CITY'S FIRST inhabited neighborhood facing the Atlantic Ocean. Rio had traditionally grown up around Guanabara Bay, but by the 1920s, the local elite began to realize that Rio could be a large capital and a beachfront resort at the same time. The Copacabana Palace Hotel, built in 1923, provided the appropriate ambience and décor for the world's high society to discover the city. The beach acquired an international reputation and, between the 1940s and the 1960s, a two-mile-long wall of apartment buildings was erected, fronting on a view that never fails to seduce.

This apartment occupies the top two floors of a building as famous for its generous proportions as for its distinguished residents, one of whom, Tancredo Neves, became the President of Brazil. In 1978 Ambassador Walther Moreira Salles and his wife, Lucia Curia Moreira Salles, hired architect Aurélio Martinez Flores and asked him to reinvent the spaces of the penthouse. They worked closely together, fulfilling the maxim that the best architecture is achieved when both the architect and the client know what they want.

Martinez Flores is the most respected minimalist architect in Brazil, a country he adopted almost thirty years ago. He started his career in his native Mexico, where he eventually worked with Mies van der Rohe. In this project he exhibits Mies' obsession with detail. Martinez Flores has a reputation for handling light with enormous talent, even in rainy São Paulo, where some of his best buildings can be found. This apartment was his first major project in Rio.

The entrance hall is covered with black marble. All the other rooms are white, which serves to frame not only the blue vista of sky meeting water but also to enhance the magnificent paintings, furniture, and objects chosen by Walther and Lucia Moreira Salles. As you go up the stairs, you discover a more relaxed atmosphere dominated by a large terrace where the entrancing views are completely unencumbered. Over the last two decades the Moreira Salles transformed this apartment into a landmark which welcomes visitors from all over the world.

In the library stand a Louis XV table and a Dom José style chair, both eighteenth-century pieces. Between the important first editions of favorite authors of Walther and Lucia Moreira Salles are seventh-century Iranian ceramics.

The terrace has a splendid view of the Copacabana beach.
Architect Martinez Flores designed the apartment in 1978.

A table prepared for lunch.

RIGHT
Light enters the room on the top floor, softened by the trellises designed by Martinez Flores. At the back, a sculpture by Sérgio Camargo.

FOLLOWING PAGES
Martinez Flores chose a minimalist approach believing in the famous Mies van der Rohe principle: "Less is more."

MAGALHÃES LINS GARDEN

White lilies and philodendrons are part of an extraordinary variety of flowers and plants in this garden, located in the district of Alto da Boa Vista.

RIGHT
The stream flowing through the property forms a natural pool created by the landscape artist Roberto Burle Marx, who designed this garden in 1974.

THIS GARDEN in the district of Alto da Boa Vista, designed in 1974 for José Luis and Nininha Magalhães Lins, is considered one of the masterpieces of Brazilian landscape architect Roberto Burle Marx, indisputably one of the most influential garden designers of the twentieth century. The house, built more than two hundred years ago, has no visible facade. It is dominated by the roof, which barely allows the visitor to notice a large terrace. Although the roof gives the house personality and charm, the star of this property is the garden.

From his first major project, the Ministry of Health and Education in Rio (1936–38), until his death in 1994, Burle Marx's name has been synonymous with beautiful gardens in Brazil. He worked on many projects with the most important architects in Brazil and his extraordinary sense of scale allowed him to create successful designs of any size—from public parks to private gardens. A retrospective of his career was organized by The Museum of Modern Art in New York in 1991.

The Magalhães Lins garden is particularly remarkable because of the contrast Burle Marx created between the natural landscape and the designed landscape. Unlike most of Burle Marx's projects, this garden did not start with carefully drawn plans. Instead, he chose to adopt a completely visual approach. Three elements had to dominate the composition: the forest, the stream that flows through the property, and the roof line of the house. Where the forest ended, Burle Marx introduced a large grass area. He then created another abrupt contrast by accentuating the banks of the river with stones and plants, as if the forest was dominant again. Then, almost imperceptibly, as the river approaches the house, it becomes a natural swimming pool, lined with granite.

Nininha's family, the Nabucos, mostly remembered for their involvement in politics and diplomacy, were also active supporters of Brazilian modern artists. Some of Nininha's relatives helped Burle Marx become a legend, so it is no surprise that he executed for the Magalhães Lins couple what is probably his best mature work.

A hidden lake surrounded by giant ferns and *bananeiras-d'água*

Burle Marx used a series of large stones found on the property, creating subtle contrasts between the native vegetation and the intervention of man.

RIGHT
The access and the bottom of the pool are covered in granite. Despite the presence of some flowers, such as different colored lilies, this major work of Burle Marx fascinates because of the seemingly infinite palette of greens here visible.

A House in São Conrado

The house of Betsy Salles Monteiro de Carvalho, designed in 1992 by Cláudio Bernardes. Behind the house, the Pedra da Gávea hill.

RIGHT
The ocean as seen from the garden.

THE BUILDING OF NEW TUNNELS AND VIADUCTS in Rio de Janeiro has led to the integration of the city with districts previously considered remote. One of them, São Conrado, is a small area with a relatively short stretch of beach surrounded by hills with exuberant vegetation. Until the 1970s there were only a few houses and the Gávea Golf Club. But today the scene has changed; the wide avenue along the sea front has been taken over by a series of elegant residential buildings making São Conrado one of the most exclusive neighborhoods of Rio de Janeiro.

It was on one of the lovely hills of the district that Betsy Salles Monteiro de Carvalho decided to build her residence, aware that in no other part of the city would the sea and the tropical vegetation both be so close. Betsy entrusted the project to Claudio Bernardes, one of Brazil's most talented new architects. Bernardes, who died in 2001, was the favorite of the young *cariocas* who built their houses in the 1990s. His architecture was both sensitive to environmental issues and faithful to Brazilian modernism. In spite of its apparent location in the middle of a forest, Bernardes designed this house as an urban dwelling. The virtual elimination of walls was achieved by suspending the house on a metal structure. The result is that the garden and the views can be appreciated from all the rooms.

Betsy and her four daughters use the house year round. Because they entertain frequently the architecture and the interior design had to accommodate the mix of generations that characterizes their social life. Betsy's father, Aloysio Salles, one of the founders of the city's Museum of Modern Art, was an esteemed intellectual and political figure in Rio. Her mother, American-born Peggy Healey Salles, introduced Brazil to her friends in the international art world. Betsy has inherited her parent's passion for the new and she is a strong supporter of contemporary artists. Her house today is a meeting place for artists, curators and art critics.

In the living room, the sculpture *Eixo Exógeno, Betsy* by Tunga, one of the most respected contemporary Brazilian artists.

RIGHT
In the entry hall, a tapestry by Joan Miró that belonged to Betsy's father, Aloysio Salles.

The swimming pool and the sea viewed from the living room.

RIGHT
With its predominating white color, the house has an informal
and youthful character; it contains many contemporary works of art,
such as the painting by the British artist Brian Clarke.

THE MARINHO HOUSE

This house, in the district of Cosme Velho,
was bought in 1938 by Roberto Marinho, and is
surrounded by a large garden. Behind, the statue
of Christ the Redeemer on top of Corcovado hill.

RIGHT
In the library, an important Russian icon and
an eighteenth-century wooden statue, the work of
Antônio Francisco Lisboa, "o Aleijadinho," the most
important artist of the Brazilian baroque period.

ROBERTO MARINHO fell in love with this property located in the district of Cosme Velho the first time he saw it, in 1938, and he immediately bought it. He redesigned the house and called on landscape designer Roberto Burle Marx to create a modern garden. As of 1940, when he opened the doors of his new home, no other house in Rio has ever seen anything close to the number of international celebrities and heads of state that the Marinhos have hosted.

In spite of being widely known as the Brazilian media mogul, perhaps even the most powerful man in the country, the owner of the Globo TV network likes to be referred to simply as *jornalista* Roberto Marinho. His career began in 1925 when he took over control of the newspaper, *O Globo*, upon the death of his father. He was just 21 years old and knew that he had inherited a potentially very valuable legacy. Over the years, he built it up into one of the largest media groups in the world. His visionary acumen probably made it easy for Marinho to see that an unexceptional house could become a spectacular property.

As a collector, Roberto Marinho has focused on Brazilian paintings of the twentieth century, baroque sculpture and colonial silver. By the mid-1990s, he and his French-born wife, Lily de Carvalho Marinho, realized that their house had almost become a museum. In order to give their art a more coherent ambience the couple decided to renovate the property inside and out. The garden, famous for its rare plants and also for the constant presence of beautiful birds, was restored by garden designer Isabel Duprat, who based her approach on Burle Marx's original plan. Lily Marinho, a prominent business woman in her own right, created the home's new interior harmony by selecting and arranging the best of the magnificent collections she and her husband had put together. Now fully restored, the house provides an ideal setting for the intense rhythm with which the couple continues to receive friends and celebrities from all over the world.

The stairway banister was originally made for an eighteenth-century palace in northern Italy. The portrait of Lily de Carvalho Marinho is the work of Kees Van Dongen.

This 1954 painting by Cândido Portinari is one of the
many works in the collection of modern Brazilian art
set up by Roberto Marinho.

LEFT
In the living room, a tapestry by F. Robert and
two Brazilian baroque figures used as a lamp base.

In the dining room, paintings by Portinari and Guignard
and a nineteenth-century Brazilian chandelier.

RIGHT
The magnificent garden, one of the first major
projects of Roberto Burle Marx, dating from 1939.
It was recently restored by Isabel Duprat, a disciple
of this great garden designer.

THE CARNEIRO DE MENDONÇA HOUSE

The entry to the garden, unmodified over the last century, preserves an atmosphere that is very difficult to find in contemporary Rio de Janeiro.

RIGHT
Built in 1843, this house located on Rua Cosme Velho is one of the best examples of residential neoclassical architecture in the city.

THE PORTUGUESE COURT had been living in Rio de Janeiro for eight years when a group of French artists was brought to the city in 1816 to establish an art school. They were instructed to pass on the latest artistic fashions from Europe. Architect Grandjean de Montigny, who had been awarded the *Grand Prix de Rome* in 1799, was among them. He brought neoclassical architecture to Brazil, breaking with centuries of baroque tradition. José Maria Jacinto Rebelo, who designed this house, was one of those Brazilian students Grandjean lived long enough to see become a leading architect. The house was commissioned in 1843 by José Borges da Costa, an influential member of the Brazilian aristocracy during the reign of Emperor Pedro II, and is still inhabited by his descendants.

This neoclassical gem is located on Rua Cosme Velho, one block from the most exquisite square in Rio, *Largo do Boticário*. Luiz Philippe and Candida Carneiro de Mendonça, who live in the house with their two children, have remained faithful to an ambience that most people believe has long been lost. They were inspired both by their families' traditions and by their belief that preserving the spirit of the house would reward them with a unique quality of life.

The house was restored in 1944 by Luiz Philippe's grandmother, Anna Amélia Queiroz, a direct descendent of Borges da Costa. She was one of the first influential feminists in Brazil, and a respected poet who translated Shakespeare's plays into Portuguese. For decades the intellectual and social elite of Rio de Janeiro made her home their favorite stamping ground. Her husband, Marcos Carneiro de Mendonça was a cult figure in Rio. He was not only the brilliant goalkeeper of the Brazilian national soccer team in the 1910s and 1920s, but also a renowned intellectual who specialized in Portuguese-Brazilian history.

Luiz Philippe, a talented young artist, and his wife felt free to have their house reflect a kind of Brazilian "shabby chic." Family portraits, eighteenth-century furniture, contemporary art, and numerous scattered books give the place an extraordinary appeal. Nothing that is necessary for modern life is missing, but comfort never outranks beauty and charm.

In a corner of the garden stands this small eighteenth-century stone fountain, brought from the city of Ouro Branco in the state of Minas Gerais.

RIGHT
This living room, with portraits of Brazilian monarchs and the Queiroz and Carneiro de Mendonça families, was for many decades a meeting place for the social and intellectual elite of Rio de Janeiro.

The portrait of José Borges da Costa, first owner of
the house, and a chair of black Brazilian rosewood
made by the French cabinet-maker Julian Béranger,
who set up in the city of Recife in 1826.

RIGHT
In the main bedroom, an eighteenth-century Brazilian
bed and trunk. Above the Brazilian rosewood bed lies
a work by Luiz Philippe Carneiro de Mendonça.

The corner of a room now used for storage.

LEFT
Luiz Philippe Carneiro de Mendonça set up his artist's studio
in the attic of the house. On the table is a portrait he made of
Candida, his wife. In the back stands an ancient bust of the
prominent eighteenth-century Portuguese Marquis de Pombal.

The gallery invaded by native plants of the Atlantic Forest.

LEFT

In this small sitting room used mostly for luncheons,
a portrait of Dedé, the nanny of Anna Amelia Queiroz.

THE MODESTO LEAL HOUSE

The main entrance to the house built
in 1892 by Count Modesto Leal,
an ancestor of the present owners.

RIGHT
The main living room maintains
the original decoration.

THIS HOUSE IS LOCATED IN LARANJEIRAS, an area where many mansions were built from the mid-nineteenth century onwards. In the 1920s and 1930s, some of them were bought by foreign governments to become residences for Ambassadors. But with the tendency of *cariocas* in the 1960s to move to apartments close to the beaches, and with the transfer of the diplomatic corps to Brasília in the 1970s, the profile of the neighborhood changed. The Modesto Leal house is one of the few great mansions of the area that still survives.

Count João Leopoldo Modesto Leal bought this property in 1892 and asked architect Antonio Januzzi to create a somewhat Italianate house. At that time architecture from the colonial period was seen as a symbol of a "dark age" in which the country was exploited by a European power and its economic system was based on slavery. Republican Brazil was eager to establish its own personality. Some colonial buildings even suffered a "facelift" with ornamentation added to facades to hide Portuguese roots. This eclectic period of Brazilian architecture—of which this house is an excellent example—lasted until the 1930s, when neocolonial and modern architecture became the favorites of the Brazilian elite.

The Leals continue to use this house as the center of family life. Wedding ceremonies still take place in the private chapel and the large reception rooms can accommodate hundreds of guests. The original décor has been preserved and reveals the predominance of French taste in interiors in Brazil at the time the house was built.

The house can be seen from the street, behind a beautiful iron fence. It is difficult, however, to imagine how large the garden is. It extends to the top of a hill from which one can enjoy one of the most beautiful views of Rio. Located in this parklike setting is an immense, empty birdcage, designed by Januzzi, which recalls the times when it was thought nature had to be controlled to be made more beautiful. This seems especially ironic in a city where nature has always been dominant.

An ancient birdcage in the garden.

LEFT
View of the house designed by architect Januzzi, in the traditional district of Laranjeiras.

The porte-cochère was added in
1908.

The stairway up to the bedrooms
is typical of late nineteenth-
century Brazilian houses.

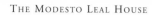

The views from the garden, surrounded by
vegetation, recall the old prints of the city
of Rio de Janeiro.

A BEACH HOUSE NEAR PARATY

The facade of the house built in 1995 by architect
Sig Bergamin, close to the colonial city of Paraty.

RIGHT
In the living room, furniture and objects of different
origins are all adapted to the beach ambiance.

THE NEW WORLD had a strong impact on European art from the seventeenth to the nineteenth centuries. Images of "savages," wild animals, and exotic plants abounded in paintings, prints, tapestries, furniture, silverware and porcelain. However, most of these works reflected the imagination of the artists, since very few had ever traveled to the Americas. Some important artists did visit Brazil during this period, and their works have helped define the country's identity. Frans Post, a Dutch painter, traveled to Brazil's northeast—Pernambuco—with an expedition led by Mauritz of Nassau in 1637. He was the first artist trained in Europe to paint *in loco* views of America.

Architect and interior designer Sig Bergamin paid tribute to some of these foreign artists in his project for this house on the coast between Rio and São Paulo, near Paraty. He was also influenced by the inevitable Portuguese contribution to Brazilian taste. But he decided to expand the concept and look for inspiration in the entire Portuguese Empire which, until the early nineteenth century, included not only Brazil but also important dominions in Africa and Asia.

The young couple who asked Bergamin to design this house in 1995 live in São Paulo, Brazil's largest city, which has a more formal lifestyle than Rio. They enthusiastically supported the architect's search for a design that would reflect the traditional Brazilian interior combined with the ambiance of a house by the sea. The couple loved antiques and old masters, but placing them in a beach house would be quite odd.

The architect and the owners of the house took the risk of reproducing old views of Brazil in some of the rooms of the house. These modern versions of works by artists who visited Brazil in the past have all been painted on a much larger scale than the originals. The house also incorporates traditional Portuguese ceramic tiles, and many pieces of furniture made of tropical woods. Bergamin took all the elements that usually create a sophisticated Brazilian interior and used them in an informal way, with talent and humor.

The gallery, facing the pool, surrounded by tropical vegetation.

In the hall, old Portuguese ceramic tiles
and tropical plant engravings.

RIGHT
Fine pieces of feathered art created by Indians
from the Amazon Basin hang next to a large-scale
reproduction of an ancient view of Brazil.

The house is located in front of a canal, a few meters from the sea. The surrounding Atlantic Forest is well preserved and strictly protected.

A House by the Sea

Built by the seashore in the State of Rio de Janeiro, this house was designed by architects Henrique Reinach and Mauricio Mendonça. They created a decidedly contemporary work while incorporating reminiscences of colonial architecture. The gallery's structure is made of huge eucalyptus trunks.

The main entry to the house.

The stairway leading to the bedrooms shows
the architects' talent and restraint.

THE COAST OF BRAZIL between Rio and São Paulo still maintains areas that have preserved the original vegetation of the *Mata Atlántica*, the exuberant tropical forest that bordered all the lengthy beaches when the first Portuguese colonizers arrived. This house is located in a residential community that promotes the integration of houses with nature and requires the use of materials that were employed in the colonial architecture of the region.

The architects Henrique Reinach and Mauricio Mendonça took these architectural limitations as a source of inspiration. The roof design appears to have been influenced by dwellings from the colonial period in the small, nearby town of Paraty. This project was commissioned by a young couple in São Paulo seeking a weekend residence with great and noble spaces, affording maximum contact with the wide-ranging natural beauty that can be viewed from the house.

To keep the apparent scale small, the house is constructed in three blocks. The main block contains the living and dining rooms and the *varanda*, with direct access to the beach. Large eucalyptus trunks were used for the structure, giving the building a decidedly modern look, which is balanced by a rattan roof cover that accentuates the beach house element. The private and service quarters occupy the other two blocks. They were designed to be more discreet, but they give the right scale to the main block. The project shows that colonial architecture is still a source of inspiration for some contemporary Brazilian architects.

The interior contains pieces from Morocco and Indonesia mixed with Brazilian furniture and objects. The owners always kept in mind the informality of a Brazilian weekend house and the climate of Rio's southern coast. By mixing tropical furniture from three different continents they obtained an unusual unity. The house as a whole reflects the ability of the architects and their clients to create a contemporary home that respects its glorious surroundings.

The swimming pool is located
just a few yards from the sea.

The Orleans e Bragança House

The entrance hall to the house at Paraty, where
Prince Dom João and Princess Dona Thereza
de Orleans e Bragança reside.

RIGHT
The first references to this building date from 1670.
Following on the local tradition of painting frames
and moldings in bright colors, Prince Dom João
chose the colors of the Brazilian flag for his house.

PARATY, located one hundred sixty miles south of Rio de Janeiro, was an important colonial town in the mid-seventeenth century. Gold mined in the hills of the state of Minas Gerais was first carried by land to Paraty's port and then sent by ship to Rio de Janeiro. But a new road built in 1704 created a direct route from the mines to the port of Rio. Paraty lost one of its main sources of revenue and in spite of its other economic activities—mainly sugar cane and coffee—the city slipped into decline. Over the years the city was forgotten. Its handsome seventeenth- and eighteenth-century buildings and squares became frozen in time.

Paraty was "rediscovered" in the 1930s with the renewed interest in colonial architecture. This house is one of the very few in Paraty that faces the ocean. Prince Dom João de Orleans e Bragança bought it in 1959. Dom João is a grandson of Princess Isabel, Emperor Dom Pedro II's daughter. He was born in France while the Brazilian Imperial family was in exile, and grew up in the castle of his grandfather, the Count d'Eu. His sister, Dona Isabel, married the heir to the French crown and became the Countess of Paris.

When he eventually moved to Brazil, Dom João became a pilot in Brazil's Marine Air Force during World War II. He later settled in Paraty and became a leading producer of *cachaça*, a raw rum made from cane alcohol. Dom João and his wife, Princess Dona Thereza, live most of the year in Paraty. This is not a weekend house for them. The couple wanted to avoid a formal interior which would not be geared to their life in Paraty. They chose to use only a few items from the Orleans e Bragança collections. These pieces, however, keep alive the spirit of Brazil's monarchy.

Dom João's son, also called João but known as Joãozinho, likewise was attracted by Paraty's charm. Joãozinho and his wife, Stella—a successful architect in Rio—recently transformed one of the town's old houses into a small hotel, the *Pousada do Príncipe*.

On a seventeenth-century wall hangs a portrait of King D. João VI—ancestor of the present owner of the house—who transferred the Portuguese court to Rio de Janeiro in 1808.

The window of this bedroom reflects the influence
of the Chinese style on Portuguese baroque architecture.

LEFT
In the access to the living room, a portrait of Blanche
d'Orléans, godmother of the owner of the house, and
in the back a portrait of D. Pedro I, Emperor of Brazil.

Sítio A Tartaruga

The serenity of the Bay of Angra dos Reis, viewed from this beach house totally surrounded by tropical vegetation.

RIGHT
Simplicity and informality characterize the property that Vivi Nabuco created out of a small fisherman's hut.

In the garden, near one of the houses, an old bamboo forest.

LEFT
Extraordinary charm is achieved by Vivi Nabuco with unpretentious decorative elements.

RIO DE JANEIRO'S MAGICAL AMBIENCE is due, in part, to its combination of a big city's business and cultural life with the informality of a town by the sea. But Rio is not a beach resort. In fact, many *cariocas* prefer to decamp on weekends to peaceful villages and isolated beaches.

This house is located about one hundred miles south of Rio, in Angra dos Reis—the Bay of Kings—a magnificent bay filled with small islands, where most houses are built in a manner that protects the forest. Access to many properties is only possible by boat. Angra dos Reis looks pretty much the way it did when it was discovered in 1502. On board the Portuguese ship that first sailed into the bay was the Italian navigator, Amerigo Vespucci, after whom the whole continent was named. Vespucci wrote rapturous encomiums to the region's beauty, but doubted the readers of his report would believe his words.

When Vivi Nabuco acquired *A Tartaruga* in 1973, there was only an old fisherman's house on the property. Endowed with the characteristics of the small buildings in Angra, this house was the main building in *A Tartaruga* for more than twenty years. With the passage of time, Vivi bought some neighboring properties where she built houses for her children and guests. With the assistance of the architect Ronaldo Fontainha and her daughter Sylvia, Vivi finally built her ideal beach house in 1995. Landscape designer Fernando Chacel was responsible for the gardens; he favored flora he found exploring the forests of the area.

Vivi is a daughter of José and Maria do Carmo Nabuco. Her parents played a central role in Brazilian politics and cultural life for decades, and she grew up surrounded by fascinating personalities. Vivi is one of the most respected businesswomen in Brazil today. Rio is not only the city where she has lived all her life; it is also her work place. A Tartaruga is her refuge, offering a complete contrast to the daily routine of her life in the great city; a place where she can truly rest at the end of the week.

This path, leading downhill to the beach,
links the different houses on the property.

LEFT
One of the houses built by Vivi Nabuco
preserving the native Atlantic Forest.

PALÁCIO GRÃO-PARÁ

Prince Dom Pedro Gastão de Orleans e Bragança
in the charming gallery of Grão-Pará where he lives
with his wife, Princess Dona Esperanza de Borbón.

RIGHT
In the entrance hall, furniture belonging to the
Brazilian Imperial family. On a Dom José style
secrètaire, along with the guest book, stands
a photograph of Queen Amélia of Portugal,
godmother of Princess D. Esperanza.

T HE EMPEROR OF BRAZIL, Dom Pedro II, began building his summer capital—Petrópolis—in the mountains, sixty miles northwest of Rio, in the 1840s. Dom Pedro wanted to be away from Rio's summer heat, in a city that would allow a comfortable, formal social life. By 1856, when the Imperial Palace was finished, many members of the aristocracy had built their houses there. Dom Pedro II was deposed in 1889 and the Brazilian Imperial Family departed for Europe.

In 1922, years after the Emperor's death, the Imperial Family was allowed to return to Brazil and recover some of their properties—among which was the Palácio Grão-Pará, not far from the Imperial Palace. Grão-Pará, built in the 1850s, was originally used as a guest house for members of the Government who would come to Petrópolis to work for a few days. It is now the residence of Prince Dom Pedro Gastão de Orleans e Bragança and his wife, Dona Esperanza de Borbón, the aunt of King Juan Carlos of Spain.

There have always been strong links between the Brazilian Imperial Family and European courts. Dom Pedro II was the son of Brazil's first Emperor, Dom Pedro I, a Bragança, the son of the Portuguese King. His mother, Empress Dona Leopoldina, was a Hapsburg, the daughter of the Emperor of Austria. Dom Pedro II married Princess Teresa Cristina, the sister of the King of Naples and his heiress, Princess Isabel, married the Count d'Eu, an Orléans, the grandson of the last French King, Louis Philippe. In spite of still being very close to European aristocracy, most of the Orleans e Braganças have adopted a low-key Brazilian way of life.

Dom Pedro Gastão, great-grandson of Dom Pedro II, and Dona Esperanza, spend their time between Grão-Pará and the Royal Palace of Villamanrique, in Seville, Spain. The objects and furniture preserved at Grão-Pará are both exceptional and significant from an historical point of view. The collection of nineteenth-century photographs of Brazil that belonged to Emperor Dom Pedro II, for example, is housed here. This house has extraordinary charm and fully reflects the elegance and dignity of Dom Pedro and Dona Esperanza.

Overlooking the garden, a view of the neoclassical facade.

RIGHT
In the main hall, a nineteenth-century screen, and mirrors that were originally in the bedroom of Empress D. Teresa Cristina, at the Imperial Palace in Rio de Janeiro.

Eighteenth-century furniture and objects were put together in this
room, some of which were brought from Portugal when the Royal
Court was transferred from Lisbon to Rio de Janeiro.

RIGHT
Photographs of Emperor D. Pedro II and Empress D. Teresa Cristina.
The French clock was brought by Princess D. Esperanza from the
Royal Palace of Villamanrique, her home in Seville, Spain.

In the entrance hall, portraits of Prince
D. Pedro Gastão and Princess D. Esperanza
painted in 1945 by Eduardo Malta.

LEFT
Photographs and memorabilia of the
Brazilian Imperial family and the Spanish
Royal family.

FAZENDA CAMPESTRE

The main entrance to the house shows the preference of architect José Zanine Caldas for natural materials, such as stones quarried from the local mountains.

RIGHT
The house at Fazenda Campestre, with the extraordinary backdrop of the Pedra dos Três Picos.

NOVA FRIBURGO, a small mountain city located one hundred miles northeast of Rio, is one of the areas where *cariocas* love to go in the summer when they want to escape Rio's heat. Beginning in the 1950s, Candido Guinle de Paula Machado, an important banker and publisher, and his wife, Maria Cecília Pedrosa, were accustomed to visiting relatives in the region. Drawn by the natural beauty of the place, where the Atlantic forest was still largely untouched, they decided to buy a piece of land with a beautiful view of the Pedra dos Três Picos mountain. In 1975, they made up their minds to build a house on their property.

The couple entrusted the project to José Zanine Caldas, a talented creator of rustic-style architecture, and suggested he seek inspiration in the Park Hotel, a small hotel in Nova Friburgo designed in the 1940s by architect Lucio Costa and destined to become one of the most influential buildings in Brazil. Zanine, a self-taught architect, was responsible in the 1970s for a new trend in Brazilian architecture. He wanted to create modern spaces using traditional materials, instead of concrete and steel. He shocked many of his colleagues by using doors and windows he found in old houses about to be demolished. But his clients were satisfied and, as his projects proliferated, a new generation of architects was influenced by his creations.

This house, one of Zanine's most acclaimed projects, was developed in close collaboration with Maria Cecília and Jorge Hue, an architect responsible for many beautiful residential projects in Brazil, including the Paula Machado house in Rio. Hue was known for his active participation in the movement for the preservation of Brazil's architectural heritage. He is committed to the idea that as long as quality is a common denominator, diversity can enrich an environment. Thus he was able to translate Zanine to Candido and Maria Cecília and vice versa. Fazenda Campestre is probably a unique case of perfect collaboration between outstanding talents and strong personalities.

Built in 1980, the house successfully combines elements of Portuguese colonial architecture with a modern structure.

The wooden structure helps to create a pleasant atmosphere
in the living room. The banisters of the upper gallery are of
the eighteenth century and the columns once belonged to
a nineteenth-century coffee warehouse.

Family souvenirs, including a photograph of the brothers
Francisco and Candido Guinle de Paula Machado.

RIGHT
Wild hydrangeas on the banks of a creek that flows
through the estate.

The exuberant vegetation is mainly due to
the rivers and streams that come down from
the mountains and flow across the property.

RIGHT
Jersey cows provide the milk used for cheese
production on the estate.

Bibliography

Library of a penthouse in the Flamengo district. The portrait, by Rafael de Madrazo, is of the Marquis Pedro Prat de Nantouillet. In the foreground, the Oscar and Anna Maria Niemeyer "Rio" Chaise Lounge, ca. 1978.

Adams, Willian Howard. *Burle Marx*. New York: The Museum of Modern Art, 1991.

Bardi, Pietro Maria. *The Arts in Brazil*. Milan: Edizioni del Milione, 1956.

Bazin, Germain. *A arquitetura religiosa barroca no Brasil*. Rio de Janeiro: Editora Record, 1983.

Beirão, Nirlando and Reinés, Tuca. *Claudio Bernardes*. São Paulo: DBA Artes Gráficas, 1999.

Bishop, Elizabeth. *Brazil*. New York: Time Inc., 1962.

Callado, Antonio. *Portinari*. Buenos Aires: Banco Velox, 1997.

Castro Maya, Raimundo de. *A muito leal e heróica Cidade de São Sebastião do Rio de Janeiro*. Rio de Janeiro: Raimundo de Castro Maya, 1965.

Cavalcanti, Lauro. *Quando o Brasil era moderno. Guia de arquitetura 1928-1960*. Rio de Janeiro: Aeroplano, 2001.

Cony, Carlos Heitor (ed.). *Rio 92*. Rio de Janeiro: Bloch Editores, 1991.

Corrêa do Lago, Pedro. *O olhar distante*. São Paulo: Associação Brasil 500 Anos - Artes Visuais, 2000.

Costa, Lucio. *Lucio Costa: registro de uma vivência*. São Paulo: Empresa das Artes, 1995.

Coustet, Robert (ed.). *Grandjean de Montigny*. Boulogne Billancourt: Bibliothèque Marmottan, 1988.

Czajkowski, Jorge (org). *Guia de arquitetura moderna no Rio de Janeiro*. Rio de Janeiro: Editora Casa da Palavra, 2000.

Evenson, Norma. *Two Brazilian Capitals*. New Haven: Yale University Press, 1973.

Fernandes Júnior, Rubens and Corrêa do Lago, Pedro. *O século XIX na fotografia brasileira*. São Paulo: Fundação Armando Álvares Penteado, 2001.

Ferreira da Silva, Suely. *Zanine*. Rio de Janeiro: Agir Editora, 1991.

Fortuna, Felipe. *Curvas, ladeiras, bairro de Santa Teresa*. Rio de Janeiro: Topbooks, 1998.

Goodwin, Philip. "Brazil Builds for the New World". *California Arts and Architecture*, Issue 60, february 1943.

Goodwin, Philip and Kidder-Smith, G.E. *Brazil Builds: Architecture old and new, 1652-1942*. New York: The Museum of Modern Art, 1943.

Hitchcock, Henry Russell. *Architecture: Nineteenth and Twentieth Centuries*. Baltimore: Penguin Books, 1958.

Kubler, George and Soria, Martin. *Art and Architecture in Spain and Portugal and their American Dominions, 1550 to 1800*. Baltimore: Penguin Books, 1959.

Martinez Flores, Aurelio. *Aurelio Martinez Flores: Arquitetura*. São Paulo: BEÎ Comunicação, 2001.

Martins, Carlos. *Museus Castro Maya*. Rio de Janeiro: Agir, 1994.

Mindlin, Henrique. *Modern Architecture in Brazil*. New York: Reinhold, 1956.

Nijinsky, Romola. Préface by Paul Claudel. *Nijinsky*. Paris: Denoel et Steele, 1934.

The Journal of Decorative and Propaganda Arts. Brazil Theme Issue. Miami: The Wolfson Foundation of Decorative and Propaganda Arts, 1995.

Tsiomis, Yamis. *Le Corbusier. Rio de Janeiro, 1929-1936*. Rio de Janeiro: Prefeitura da Cidade do Rio de Janeiro, 1998.

Underwood, David. *Niemeyer*. New York: Rizzoli, 1994.

Vasquez, Pedro and Silva Telles, Augusto. *Rio de Janeiro 1862-1927*. São Paulo: Instituto Moreira Salles, 1998.

Wethey, Harold E. *Alonso Cano. Pintor, escultor y arquitecto*. Madrid: Alianza Editorial, 1983.

Zanini, Walter (ed.). *História geral da arte no Brasil*. São Paulo: Instituto Moreira Salles, 1983.

Acknowledgments

WE WOULD LIKE TO THANK all those who have so generously allowed their houses to be photographed. Always we were made to feel welcome and comfortable. Very special thanks to Theresa Muniz, who supported the project from the beginning and offered her valuable and expert opinion and to our friend André Corrêa do Lago, who took an extraordinarily personal interest in the book and suggested great ideas.

We would particularly like to thank the following individuals, all of whom have contributed to the development of this book, in one way or another: Lucia Moreira Salles, Dawber Gontijo, Béatrice Corrêa do Lago, João Mauricio de Araujo Pinho, Vivi Nabuco, Carlos Lins e Silva, Perla Mattison, Reinaldo and Carolina Herrera, Lily de Carvalho Marinho, Helô Guinle, Tite de Lamare, Pablo Larreta and Carmen de Iriondo, Yvonne Muniz, Tana Pujals, Pedro and Beatriz Corrêa do Lago, Manoel and Izabel Corrêa do Lago, Beatriz Larragoiti, Countess Emita de Pourtalès, Olavo Monteiro de Carvalho, Helio and Sylvia Fraga, Prince and Princess D. Pedro Carlos de Orleans e Bragança, Prince D. Joãozinho de Orleans e Bragança, Beatriz Pimenta Camargo, Beatrizinha Monteiro de Carvalho, Tania Salem Derani, Emilio Kalil, Romaric Sulger Büel, Eduardo Figueiredo, José de Paula Machado, Jorge Hue, René Haguenauer, Alcides Guimarães, José Francisco Gouvêa Vieira, Patricia Leal, Antonio Neves da Rocha, Antonio Pedro Bocayuva, María Cristina Monterubbianesi, Lolly Hime, Luiz Fernando Secco, Eduardo Ayerza, Edgar Peixoto, Luisa de Alzaga, Paulette Villanueva and Ivan Stocker-Rakolczay.

Our thanks also go to Roa Lynn, Sarah Jane Freymann, Sula Danowski, Adriana Cataldo, Alberto Flaksman, Rosalina Gouveia, Gustavo Lacerda and Luiza Gray. At BEI Comunicação, thanks to Marisa Moreira Salles, Tomas Alvim, Ana Helena Vicintin, Cecília Sicupira, Lucia Yumi Saneshigue, Tatiana de Moraes and Américo Freiria. At the Instituto Moreira Salles, we thank Antonio Fernando De Franceschi, Odette Vieira, Elizabeth Pessoa Teixeira and Cristina Zappa. At Fundação Estudar, thanks to Carlos Martins and Valéria Piccoli.

In New York, at Rizzoli International Publications, we are especially grateful to David Morton and Douglas Curran.

Juan Pablo Queiroz e Tomás de Elia

Illustration Credits